What Christians Should Know About…

A Personal Relationship with God

Peter Nodding

Sovereign World

Copyright © 1997 Peter Nodding

All rights reserved. No part of this publication may be reproduced,
stored in a retrieval system, or transmitted in any form or by any means,
electronic, mechanical, photocopying, recording or otherwise,
without the prior written consent of the publisher.

Short extracts may be quoted for review purposes.

Unless otherwise stated in the text, all Scripture quotations are
taken from the HOLY BIBLE, NEW INTERNATIONAL VERSION.
© Copyright 1973, 1978, 1984 International Bible Society.
Used by permission.

ISBN: 1 85240 216 4

This Sovereign World book is distributed in North America by Renew Books,
a ministry of Gospel Light, Ventura, California, USA. For a free catalog of resources
from Renew Books/Gospel Light, please contact your Christian supplier
or call 1-800-4-GOSPEL.

SOVEREIGN WORLD LIMITED
P.O. Box 777, Tonbridge, Kent TN11 0ZS, England.

Typeset and printed in the UK by Sussex Litho Ltd, Chichester, West Sussex.

About the Author

Peter Nodding leads the Church at the Millmead Centre in Guildford. He was previously at West Bridgford Baptist Church, Nottingham, and in both places several new congregations have been planted.

Before entering the pastoral ministry he worked as an evangelist for five years with Cliff College, a Bible college in Derbyshire, England.

Originally a Methodist, now a Baptist Pastor and trained at a Church of England theological college (St John's College, Nottingham), he believes his life has been enriched through the diversity of these traditions.

Peter has a wider ministry in teaching and encouragement of leaders and is particularly committed to Word and Spirit ministry and the unity of God's people. He is married with two teenage children.

Contents

	Introduction	7
1	Starting Well	9
2	God's Priority	15
3	Under Pressure	21
4	Being Sure	25
5	Two Keys	33
6	When Tested	41

Dedication

To my daughter, Catherine.

Introduction

Several years ago, when I was Pastor of an English Church, a group of us surveyed the community with a questionnaire. After we had introduced ourselves we asked if they would answer 10 questions, five about the community and five about Christianity. We were generally warmly received.

Question 10 was "If you could know God personally would you want to know Him?" Most people answered with these words, "Well, yes, but you can't know Him, can you?"

It is tragic that the Christian Church has not communicated this basic fact. So many just do not know what is on offer. Most people think Christianity is about morality or being religious, rather than about having a relationship with God. In these chapters I have included a lot of Scripture because I want to allow the Bible to speak for itself. What do the writers of the New Testament say?

> *"Now this is eternal life: that they may know you, the only true God, and Jesus Christ whom you have sent."*
> (John 17:3 – Jesus Christ the Son of God)

> *"I want to know Christ and the power of his resurrection."*
> (Philippians 3:10 – The Apostle Paul)

> *"Though you have not seen him, you love him; and even though you do not see him now, you believe in him and are filled with an inexpressible and glorious joy."*
> (1 Peter 1:8 – The Apostle Peter)

> *"We know that we have come to know him if we obey his commands."* (1 John 2:3 – The Apostle John)

This book invites us to go deeper into our knowledge of God. As well as encouraging people to make a start, I have mainly concentrated on those aspects which will bring the greatest maturity. As you read on, may God *"give you the Spirit of wisdom and revelation, so that you may know him better."* (Ephesians 1:17)

1

Starting Well

Throughout the Bible, relationship with God is variously described. Adam *knew* God, Abel *was in the right* with God, Noah *heard* God, Abraham *believed* God, Jacob *worshipped* God, Moses *relied* on God, the Priests *served* God and the Prophets *spoke from* God.

There is nothing more important than an individual's relationship with God. Discovering it and then learning how to maintain it, is to fulfil the main purpose for our existence. I am writing mainly for those who have begun to 'know the Lord', but I invite those who are searching to read on.

Julie responded to Christ's invitation to know him on the first occasion that she attended a church. She was not brought up in a Christian family, but six weeks before this she had gone into a city centre church during her lunch hour, and prayed a simple prayer. On the Sunday morning when she asked me if she could become a Christian, I realised that she was remarkably ready to respond. Julie went on to marry a man who is now a church leader.

John and Pat had been doing Bible studies with Jehovah Witnesses. During these studies they grew uneasy about some aspects of the Witness's teaching. They telephoned our church and asked for help. A few months later, after attending our services and then a short course on the basics of the Christian faith, they found a personal relationship with Christ for themselves. John and Pat continue to serve the Lord and have had the joy of helping others to come to know Christ personally.

What is relationship with God according to the Bible?

We cannot simply compare it with the relationships we have with other human beings, although there are certain similarities. The Bible teaches that the relationship is spiritual, it includes covenant, it is on the basis of repentance and faith, and is of a different – indeed incomparable – quality from all other relationships.

Spiritual

We do not relate to God through our five senses, but through our human spirit to His Holy Spirit. Our spirit is brought to life as we rightly respond to God in repentance and faith. This opens the door to the beginning of the relationship with Him, through the Holy Spirit being poured into our human spirits. We come alive towards God, whereas previously we had been dead towards Him. The Bible refers to this spiritual death as being *"dead in your transgressions and sins"* (Ephesians 2:1).

It is crucial that this spiritual dimension is understood. There are many who have a belief in God, but do not know Him because they are trying to understand Him on the basis of their five senses. As these senses are the way that we know, or become aware of things in the material world, it is natural to think that it is the same with knowing God.

You may remember the Russian cosmonaut who returned from space and triumphantly announced that he had not seen God. A little girl was reported to have said "of course not, it is only the pure in heart who see God."

We cannot see God with our natural eyes, but we can see Him with the eyes of our heart (Ephesians 1:18); we cannot hear God with our natural ears, but we can learn to hear Him as He teaches us to recognise the voice of the Holy Spirit.

I have watched the light dawning on people's faces when I have explained that I have never seen God with my physical eyes, and never heard Him with my ears, but have then gone on to explain that this doesn't mean that you cannot know Him. There are plenty of us who have begun our search by saying "If you are out there God, please reveal yourself to me." The answer to this prayer is not natural, but supernatural.

It was Jesus who explained this process clearly when He spoke of being born again of the Spirit in John's Gospel Chapter 3. We have all been born physically through the natural process of reproduction. Man's sperm and the woman's egg unite to form the embryo of new life. However, the birth from the Holy Spirit is different. Jesus calls it 'being born again' where God Himself is our Father.

My physical birth pre-dated my spiritual birth by fifteen years. The second one resulted in the beginnings of my relationship with the Heavenly Father.

The Apostle Paul write confidently that

> "God sent the Spirit of His Son into our hearts, the Spirit who calls out, 'Abba Father.'" (Galatians 4:6)

Interestingly the word used here (Abba), is the one that expresses the most intimate term within a family. We might say "Daddy".

Covenant

First of all a simple definition. A covenant is an agreement or promise made between two parties. The Bible mentions a number of covenants. In the Old Testament, God made a covenant with individuals, like Noah and Abraham; with the nation of Israel; and with King David. In the New Testament another covenant was established through Jesus Christ. Our Bible is divided into two parts, referred to as the Old and the New Testaments. The word 'testament' is another word for covenant.

In the marriage ceremony the following words are used when the rings are exchanged. "I give you this ring as a token of the covenant made between us this day and as a pledge of our mutual love." Promises of faithfulness are pledged one to the other. There is much in the marriage covenant which illustrates our relationship with God, but it is imperfect in expressing the extent of God's commitment to us.

What are the features of the old and the new covenants? God

promised that He would bless the nation of Israel in a multitude of ways, but essentially He would be in relationship with them. Israel's part was to obey the commandments and to be faithful to their one God. The chapters of the Old Testament are the sad story of how they failed to do so. In the New Testament Jesus refers to His death as making and sealing the New Covenant (Mark 14:24). He sent the Holy Spirit to the Church as a proof of it (Acts 1:4-5). God had declared and demonstrated that He was committed to us by giving us His Son as a sacrifice on the cross for our sins. I explain God's commitment to us more fully in the next chapter.

Repentance and faith

Repentance is required because each individual is in need of forgiveness. A secure relationship with God is only possible when the damage caused by the fall of man, described in Genesis 3, is repaired. Adam and Eve, who enjoyed relationship with God, chose to disobey him and the rest of us have been affected ever since.

We do not enter the world with a built-in knowledge of God, in fact just the opposite. We are, by nature, more prone to choose the wrong rather than the right. This truth is not easily accepted in a society that wants us to believe that it can improve itself by its own efforts. C.S. Lewis expressed the heart of the problem when he said, "man does not realise how bad he is until he tries to be good."

When an individual realises that he is sinful in God's sight (as a result of the conviction of the Holy Spirit), he can choose to repent – that is, turn from sin. If repentance is true, it means a real change will take place in the person. As someone once said "it is not enough to only feel sorry for sins committed, but sorry enough not to do them again."

Repentance is a much misunderstood word. A man was cheating on his income tax and as a result was unable to sleep at night. He decided to write to the Inland Revenue and enclose a cheque. After explaining his situation, he closed his letter by saying "if I still cannot sleep at night, I will send you the rest!"

True repentance is a change of heart (redirecting our affections), a change of mind (thinking differently about God and ourselves), and a change of will (choosing God's way and not our own). The repentant person agrees with God about sin and is willing to put things right with God's help.

Faith has many facets and at this stage I can only touch on it briefly. We will be considering the faith that learns to depend on God on a daily basis and the faith that grows through testing, but what of the faith that opens the door to relationship with Him?

The Bible describes this as 'saving faith'. After repentance saving faith believes in the death and resurrection of Jesus Christ. Such a person is saying "I believe that when Christ died on the cross He was doing it for me." It is saving faith because it is rescuing us from sin which, if not cleansed, leads to spiritual and eternal death. It is as though a person is drowning in the river unable to save himself, and Christ reaches down to lift him out. Faith results in a believer knowing that he is forgiven. He really believes that God is declaring him 'not guilty' in His sight.

Nothing quite like it

The Apostle Paul sums this up for us when he writes:

> *"But whatever was to my profit I now consider loss for the sake of Christ. What is more, I consider everything a loss compared to the **surpassing greatness of knowing** Christ Jesus my Lord, for whose sake I have lost all things. I consider them rubbish, that I may gain Christ and be found in him, not having a righteousness of my own based on law, but that which is through faith in Christ – the righteousness that comes from God and is by faith."* (Philippians 3:7-9)

For those who have discovered this relationship with God through Jesus Christ, we know Paul was not exaggerating.

There is nothing to compare with the privilege of being in relationship with Him through His Son, Jesus Christ. It gives us something to live for and to die for. I have heard hundreds of people say that there is no one like Jesus in their lives. For those who have received Him and begun to follow Him sincerely there is no turning back. Knowing Him has answered the fundamental questions of life's meaning.

Jesus told a couple of short parables which make this point superbly. He was talking about what the Kingdom of Heaven is like. He said:

> *"The Kingdom of Heaven is like treasure hidden in a field. When a man found it, he hid it again and then in his joy went out and sold all that he had and bought that field. Again the Kingdom of Heaven is like a merchant looking for fine pearls, when he found one of great value, he went away and sold everything he had and bought it."* (Matthew 13:44-46)

Graham Kendrick's song expresses this truth beautifully.

All I once held dear built my life upon,
All this world reveres and wars to own,
All I once thought gain I have counted loss;
Spent and worthless now compared to this.

Knowing you, Jesus, knowing you,
there is no greater thing.
You're my all, you're the best
You're my joy my righteousness.
And I love you Lord.[1]

---

[1] Graham Kendrick, Copyright © 1993. Make Way Music, PO Box 263, Croydon, Surrey, CR9 5AP. Int. copyright secured. All rights reserved. Used by permission.

2

God's Priority

I have spoken to a few people who were convinced that a particular person didn't like them. It often arises because of insecurity and certainly because of an incomplete knowledge of the third party. If they could only see the truth from the other person's point of view, they would be set free.

We must see relationship from God's perspective before our own. God's will and delight to relate to us closely immediately encourages us to be more responsive to Him. By considering a number of Old Testament verses we can see what God intended.

What has God said?

Exclusive

> *"You shall have no other gods before me."* (Exodus 20:3)

It was stated emphatically at the outset of the old covenant that God wanted an exclusive relationship with His people. God would not tolerate any rivals. Israel belonged to Him and He was rightly jealous when they replaced Him with other gods. They were to *"Love the Lord your God with all your heart and with all your soul and with all your strength."* (Deuteronomy 6:5). And to teach their children to do the same.

Steadfast love

> *"For I desire mercy, not sacrifice, and acknowledgement of God rather than burnt offerings."* (Hosea 6:6)

This particular verse is picked up by Jesus twice in Matthew's

Gospel (9:13; 12:7) and is clearly a pivotal truth for us to grasp. God is not impressed with the self-righteousness of the Pharisees, or the list of laws that bind people rather than set them free.

One of the church placements, when I was being trained as a Pastor, encouraged their members to be teetotal. I was very happy to accept this ruling at the time although I understood that the scriptural position was moderation in drinking alcohol. However, what concerned me was that some more obvious sins, like gossip, pride and self-righteousness were tolerated.

The sort of relationship that God wants is summed up in the Old Testament Hebrew word 'hesed'. It is translated variously as mercy, kindness, goodness, loving-kindness, and faithfulness. What underlies it is God's covenant love. It is often translated steadfast love, and it includes God's attitude to His people and their's to Him.

Tireless commitment

> *"You only have I chosen of all the families of the earth; therefore I will punish you for all your sins. Do two walk together unless they have agreed to do so?"* (Amos 3:2-3)

Many times God reaffirmed that He had made Israel His special choice. He had chosen to love them which was a result of His nature, not theirs. He would go the extra mile in His faithfulness, but they also needed to know that their privileges implied responsibilities. He wanted them to be like a couple who had agreed to walk together and share all that they had in common. God is tireless in His commitment to relationship.

Lasting relationship

> *"This is the covenant that I will make with the house of Israel after that time declares the Lord. I will put my law in their minds and write it on their hearts. I will be their God and they will be my people. No longer will a man teach his neighbour, or a man his brother, saying, 'know the Lord,'*

> *because they will all know me from the least of them to the greatest."* (Jeremiah 31:33-34)

It became clear that God's people would not keep His first covenant. Any stimulus that came from the Priesthood, Monarchy and Temple had failed. Jeremiah, 600 years before Jesus, saw that God would establish a new covenant (through the life, death and resurrection of Jesus), which would provide spiritual power on the inside and lead individuals into a lasting relationship with God.

This insight of Jeremiah reveals how deeply God is committed to relationship. The New Testament spells it out far more eloquently. It was at incredible cost that God purchased and ratified His relationship with us. The Apostle Peter writes:

> *"For you know it was not with perishable things such as silver and gold that you were redeemed from the empty way of life handed down to you from your forefathers, but with the precious blood of Christ, a lamb without blemish or defect."* (1 Peter 1:18-19)

God has demonstrated that He wants relationship, and the sacrifice of His Son is the final undeniable action that achieved it. We will be speaking in later chapters about our response, but let us be absolutely clear about God's love towards us. I find that many Christians stumble because they are unsure of their standing with God. They are weak in their knowledge of identity. If we are not sure of the basis of our complete acceptance by God, we will stumble.

Two things to know

The relationship has a spiritual base and so it is at the level of our human spirit where assurance should reside. If we will pray 'Lord teach me' and to say it sincerely and with openness of heart, He will give us a clear revelation of His love for us.

Knowing His affirmation
When Jesus was being baptised in the River Jordan His Father

spoke to Him. *'You are my Son, whom I love; with you I am well pleased'* (Luke 3:22). Jesus knew this truth from eternity past, but this didn't mean that it should not be expressed afresh to Him. I believe that the Holy Spirit affirms us in the Father's love over and over again. It was St Augustine who said 'God loves each person as though there is only one person to love.' *"The Spirit himself testifies with our spirit that we are God's children"* (Romans 8:16).

There is one important fact that every Christian needs to understand about affirmation. We receive it primarily from God Himself through relationship. If we look for it in human quarters, we will receive a measure of encouragement, but it is the Lord Himself who wants to affirm us in His love. Some will immediately argue that for many the only way that they will receive God's love is through a human channel. This is true. However, the principle is the same. Each of us needs to receive the revelation from God's Spirit to our spirit. It is the only way that we will be spiritually secure.

What about those who are emotionally damaged? It is tragically possible to be so hurt and damaged by the most important relationships in our lives that we are unable to enter into a strong relationship with Father God or with others in the Fellowship. Parents have been cruel or we have been rejected as children. Christians are not immune from this deep emotional pain and when we come to the Lord it is with the baggage of broken relationships and a deep mistrust of intimacy. This means that we erect barriers and protect ourselves from any further hurt.

One such person, whom I shall call Mary, shares the following testimony. "I come from a difficult background. My mother was emotionally crippled and spent time during my early years in and out of psychiatric hospitals. My father was a self-centred man, driven by his own needs who would often not speak to me for months at a time. By the time I was twelve the family had split up. What hope was there of building good relationships in such a home? My experience of relationships was that they hurt, and I ended up totally barricaded in by walls of ice that froze my emotions to stone. At twenty I married a good man but not for love; more because he cared where I had never experienced care before. In those early turbulent years of marriage I was unable to cope, not knowing how to be in a relationship. But my husband's family were Christians and they were praying.

At a low point I attended a service at a local church where the young man who sat next to me shared something of his relationship with God. I had never before heard that anyone could have a relationship with God. Surely you just believed in Him and cried out when you were desperate. Within weeks I had given my life to Jesus, but relationships were still difficult. Quite simply I needed healing.

At crisis point I sought help from the church and during a time of counselling and prayer, Jesus began to heal the broken relationship with my father. Jesus took the hurting child and brought His healing into my broken emotions. I was able to forgive my father and find release from the block of ice that had held me for so long. It was not all healed in a day, but the dramatic outcome was that I was reconciled to my father who had not wanted anything to do with me for sixteen years."

Mary's healing had a profound effect on her relationship with her Heavenly Father. It has deepened, become solid and is now the most precious thing in her life.

Knowing the power of the cross

I have been speaking of knowing affirmation at the level of experience, but what about something more objective? God had to find a way to forgive us which was righteous and just. He had previously made clear that sinful people deserved death; we see this from the opening chapters of Genesis.

The cross was the way that God remained faithful to His judgement on sin, and yet proved to be the way that sin could be forgiven.

> *"God offered him* (Jesus at the cross) *so that by his death he should become the means by which men's sins are forgiven, through their faith in him. God did this in order to demonstrate his righteousness. In the past, he was patient and overlooked men's sins, but now in the present time he deals with men's sins, to demonstrate his righteousness. In*

this way God shows that he himself is righteous and that he puts right everyone who believes in Jesus."
(Romans 3:25-26, Today's English Version)

How do I know that God will go on accepting me? Because of the cross. The death of Jesus does not just open the door to the Christian faith, but it is the foundation on which we stand. God has accepted us because of His Son. He will go on making us clean from sin, *"because the blood of Jesus his Son, purifies us* (goes on cleansing us) *from sin"* (1 John 1:7).

God can do no more. He invites us into covenant relationship. He will remain faithful and will always reward our trust in Him.

3

Under Pressure

The Bible teaches us that we are to overcome pressure from three sides, the world, the flesh and the Devil. In this chapter I am not addressing the pressures that come from outside us, namely the world and the Devil, but I want to concentrate on two areas that are in our hands and which we can do something about. God has given us the ability to make choices and our Christian growth depends on making the best ones.

I am not covering the issue of personal sin, but it must be obvious that if we choose to harbour resentments, live in unforgiveness, allow ourselves to trifle with sinful attitudes and actions, we are going to put pressure on the relationship. God has called us to be clean, and has provided the means in His Son to be washed and renewed.

Busyness

Although we have an increasing number of labour-saving devices, and the time it takes to travel from A to B is constantly decreasing, we become more, rather than less, busy. We probably manage to put twice or three times as much into a day as those who lived 100 years ago.

I recently visited Caldey Island off the coast of Wales. Almost continuously from its beginning in the sixth century, there has been some form of monastic life on the island. The simplicity of the lifestyle challenged me. Their day begins at 3.15am and ends at 8.00pm. Seven services every day, study and some form of labour (except on Sunday) fill the time.

I am not advocating the life of a monk for all, but simply reminding myself how, for most of us, our lives are cluttered. Certainly in the West busyness is the arch enemy of living close to

God. I suppose the important question to ask is – what sort of busyness is it? The life of John Wesley in the 18th century was very busy. He rose early and often preached at 5am before moving on to the next place. He wrote several books, rode thousands of miles, established hundreds of meetings, but found time to pray.

What about Jesus? Was His life busy? We clearly don't have a full picture of His days. The Gospels only provide a outline of His time on earth. We are aware of the main events, but the hours of His day are not documented in detail.

A very busy day is recorded in Capernaum at the beginning of His ministry. After the Sabbath ended at 6pm we are told that He healed all who came to Him. What time did he get to bed? The next verse reads

> *"Very early in the morning, while it was still dark, Jesus got up, left the house and went off to a solitary place, where he prayed."* (Mark 1:35)

We know of three occasions when He spent the night in prayer, but we don't know how common this was. On another occasion when He and His disciples had been busy He said, *"Come with me by yourselves to a quiet place and get some rest"* (Mark 6:31). Ironically almost as soon as they arrived at this solitary place the crowds, who had seen them depart, hurried ahead and arrived there before them. This opened the door to the feeding of the five thousand (Mark 6:32-44).

Jesus is teaching us that it is not the amount of work we do – we may well be busy – but we need to be finding quality time in prayer. It is prayer and time with the Father that is higher on Jesus' agenda than ministry. We see the pattern of His prayer and ministry from two verses.

> *"Yet the news about him spread all the more, so that crowds of people came to hear him and to be healed of their sickness. But Jesus often withdrew to lonely places and prayed."*
>
> (Luke 5:15-16)

It appears that Jesus had the freedom in His spirit to leave the crowds, even though there were pressing needs, and retreat to a place where He could renew His spiritual strength. It would also give Him clarity about what the Father wanted Him to do next. I have just mentioned the busy day in Capernaum in Mark 1:21-34. Jesus was enjoying considerable success and as far as the disciples were concerned they wanted Him to stay because the people were thrilled with Him. But after His early morning prayer-time, He had heard the Father's direction. *"Let us go somewhere else – to the nearby villages – so that I can preach there also. That is why I have come"* (Mark 1:38).

May I suggest to you that Jesus' pattern of prayer is the key to our busyness. At times He will say to us that we need to slow down and do little or no ministry, because He wants to be at **work in us**.

Arthur Wallis in his early life heard the Lord say that he wanted him to pray and study for nine months of the year and preach for three. At this stage he was a single man living at home, and so for a few years he made this commitment. Billy Graham has often said that he wished that he preached less and studied more in his earlier ministry. Charles Spurgeon said that if he knew he had twenty-five years to live he would have used twenty of them in preparation.

For some of us our secular work commitments are keeping us from reaching our full potential. The Lord is inviting us to give more time to church-related ministry. However, it is more likely that our secular employment **is** our ministry. God is using us to bring His light into darkness and we are salt amongst those with whom we work. God calls us to be teachers, accountants, civil servants, factory workers as well as preachers. It probably will be the case that when we give the right commitment to prayer and listening we will have less busy lives, as we become more concerned with the quality of what we are doing.

Lack of fellowship

We were not made to be alone in the Christian life. We have been placed in a community of faith (the Church) which is designed to provide our spiritual sustenance. Unfortunately this does not always work out in reality.

When preparing this book I asked a number of people to fill in a questionnaire. One of the questions was the subject of this chapter (i.e. what puts the relationship with God under pressure?). I discovered that for some people it was discouragement coming from fellow Christians that puts pressure on their relationship with God. I trust this is not widespread, but it reminds us that we need to invest love and encouragement into our meeting with one another, so that our brothers and sisters can be made strong.

Two packs to carry
In Galatians 6:1-6 Paul teaches us how we are to be supportive of one another. He writes *"Carry each other's burdens, and in this way you will fulfil the law of Christ"* (Galatians 6:2). We were not made to function on our own. We enter more fully into Christ as we learn to ease the load of others, and in turn allow others to carry our burdens for us. One person may be too self-sufficient whilst another may be too dependent on a fellow Christian. It is only the Holy Spirit who can teach us the right balance.

Interestingly Paul talks about another load in Galatians 6:5 where *"each one should carry his own load."* There are two different Greek words employed in verses 2 and 5. The first speaks of a heavy load, and the second a light pack on our back. There are some loads that we do need to learn to carry ourselves, and we will spoil our fellowship if we become too dependent on a fellow Christian. Again it is the Holy Spirit who will teach us what is our responsibility and what is to be shared with others.

4

Being Sure

The Bible is so practical as well as teaching spiritual truths. When we want to be sure about our standing with God we must not take our spiritual temperature in a vacuum. For the person who has begun to relate to God through repentance, forgiveness and faith, other guidelines have been given as a framework for us.

One of Jesus' disciples called John who wrote one of the Gospels, also wrote three other letters. In the first, and longest of these, he outlined four tests by which we can be sure that we know God.

The four tests appear in the second chapter of John's first Epistle. We will see that they are demanding tests and the only way that they can be adequately 'lived out' is in the power of God's Spirit. John is not trying to make things hard for his readers, he is writing to encourage them. He knows that if the Spirit of God has brought them to birth in Christ, they will want to fulfil these requirements. So what are they?

Obedience (1 John 2:3-6)

He puts it so simply and clearly.

> *"We know that we have come to know him if we keep His commands. The man who says, 'I know him,' but does not do what he commands is a liar, and the truth is not in him. But if anyone obeys his word, God's love is truly made complete in him. This is how we know we are in him: Whoever claims to live in him must walk as Jesus did."*

We are in an age when it is fashionable to disobey; whether it is parents, police, or parliament. It is so recurrent that many who have no interest in God or Christianity, often express their concern about this sort of rebellious behaviour. For those who understand the nature of sin and human weakness, it is obvious that it is an outworking of what an individual or society is like without godly constraints.

What does obedience mean?

There are three ideas that are covered in these verses.

> Obeying God's commands:- the general commands outlined in Scripture.
> Obeying His word:- the more specific words that God speaks to us that require our 'yes'.
> Behaving like Jesus Christ:- the example of Jesus in the way that He lived.

In this passage the Apostle also uses three words or phrases that describe relationship. He says we *'know Him'*. It is a key word in the first short letter and is used on 25 occasions. He speaks of having *'love for God'*, and here he means love expressed in our wills and decisions and not just our feelings. Finally he reminds us that we are *'in Him'* or are in union with Him. There is no question about it. As a result of Jesus dying and rising again we have been made one with God, we have been united to the Father in relationship.

Test number one.

Is it the case that because of your love for God you are increasingly willing to be obedient to the Lord?

Loving one another (1 John 2:7-11)

> *"Dear friends, I am not writing you a new command but an*

> *old one, which you have had since the beginning. This old command is the message you have heard. Yet I am writing you a new command; its truth is seen in him and you, because the darkness is passing and the true light is already shining."* (1 John 2:7-8)

In this section the Apostle narrows down the general commands to a specific one of loving one another. It is both an old commandment and a new one. Loving one another had been taught by Jesus and so His disciples would know it. It was also part of the Old Testament Law. (See Leviticus 19:18.)

However, it was also new. The newness was the quality that Jesus gave to it. He taught His disciples that it summed up the whole law and that they were to love one another just as He had loved them. Here was a tremendous simplicity and depth to be grasped. The scores of individual laws finding their fulfilment in loving one another.

It is so practical. By truly loving our brother we will enjoy the light and blessing of God around us, but to hate our brother is to forfeit it. Love and hate are absolute contrasts which make the point starkly.

We may think that there is no hatred in us. However, we are more deeply challenged by the underlying root meaning. Anger, annoyance and resentment are all part of the same root; sinful emotion. The result of harbouring such attitudes is to break our fellowship with God as well as our brother. The antidote is the way of confession, repentance and cleansing (1 John 1:7).

I am always challenged by Paul's word in Romans *"Be **devoted** to one another in brotherly love"* (12:10). Devotion speaks of heart involvement. The Lord Jesus spoke of lukewarmness to the Laodicean Church in Revelation. It is a positive and active loving of one another that fulfils this commandment.

We are counselled not to remain in such attitudes otherwise three things will follow.

We are placed in the darkness (v11). (The darkness is this present age or the sinful world which is opposite to the light in Jesus).

We may cause others to sin (v10). (The implication is that if we stumble we may cause others to do so as well).

The darkness causes spiritual blindness (v11).

> Test number two.
>
> Do you maintain good relationships with fellow Christians? Do you quickly put things right with them if the relationship has broken down?

Do you love the world? (1 John 2:15-17)

> *"Do not love the world or anything in the world. If anyone loves the world, the love of the Father is not in him. For everything in the world – the cravings of sinful man, the lust of the eyes and the boasting of what he has or does – comes not from the Father but from the world. The world and its desires pass away, but the man who does the will of God lives for ever."*

Let us first of all be clear what is meant by the world. John 3:16 tells us that *"God so loved the world that he gave his one and only Son."* So why should we not love it? It is the world system or the ways of the world that we are not to love. It is this aspect of the world that will *"squeeze us into its own mould"* (Romans 12:2 J B Phillips translation).

Today's English version puts v16 more clearly, explaining what the ways of the world are like:

> *"what the sinful self desires, what people see and want, and everything in this world that people are so proud of."*

What is being described is a life lived for oneself with no reference to God as Father. So the contrast is made between the ways of the world and having love for the Father. It is a clear choice between these two ways of living.

Jesus Christ is the model. He was able to demonstrate love

for worldly people (tax collectors, sinners), but without compromising His lifestyle. Pray that God will give you compassion for people in the world whoever they are, but also pray that your love for God will be strong so that you do not follow the world's ways.

Test number three.

Is your life characterised by a genuine love for God as your Father and is this enabling you to live a life increasingly free from giving in to the temptations of the world?

Knowing what you believe (1 John 2:22-23)

> *"Who is the liar? It is the man who denies that Jesus is the Christ. Such a man is the antichrist – he denies the Father and the Son. No-one who denies the Son has the Father; whoever acknowledges the Son has the Father also."*

In the early Church false teachers led believers into false doctrines about Jesus Christ. One of the reasons that John wrote His first letter was that those who had begun to believe in Jesus should remain faithful to the truth. There are two truths in particular found in the above verses.

Firstly we see that to truly believe will mean that we **honour Jesus as Messiah**. This means we recognise that He is God's anointed one (fully God and fully man), sent to be the Saviour and Lord by dying on the cross and rising again from the dead.

Secondly that **the Son and the Father are one**. Most of the false teaching in the early centuries centred around the person of Jesus. Some said He was only a very good man and not God, or that He was God but not a human being, or that He was a god, but inferior to the supreme God. Here we are told unequivocally that Jesus and the Father are one. If we don't honour Jesus we do not honour His Father.

I remember asking a class of eleven year olds in Liverpool

'what is Jesus Christ like?' One boy answered 'He is exactly like God.' A brilliant and true answer.

A member of our church in Nottingham had great difficulty singing a particular song. The words were 'Jesus is the Lord God Almighty'. She had come out of a cult that drew a distinction between Jesus and God. She felt that she was singing heresy in these words. It was when she had a deeper experience of the Holy Spirit that she found the freedom to know Jesus as one with the Father and therefore Almighty God.

This leads us to answering the question of how can we be sure of these two truths and how do we keep them alive within us? It is the ministry of the Spirit which is the key. Towards the end of chapter 2 we are told two things about the Spirit.

1. He has been poured out on us by Christ. The anointing refers to the Holy Spirit that was initially given at Pentecost. *"But you have an anointing from the Holy One, and all of you know the truth"* (1 John 2:20).

2. The Holy Spirit remains in you. The Spirit of God was active in people's lives in the Old Testament, but the difference after Pentecost was that He remained permanently in the believer. He has become the personal friend who imparts to us the truths about Jesus Christ so that we can be sure of them. *"As for you, the anointing you received from him remains in you, and you do not need anyone to teach you"* (1 John 2:27).

Christians are not people who are merely hoping for the best or simply imagine we have some good ideas about Jesus Christ. These truths have been personally written **on our hearts as the Spirit has taken up residence within us.** He is our personal teacher.

However, please don't think that you don't need any other teachers. God has placed teachers in the Church (1 Corinthians 12:28) who are able to explain God's word and build up the Body of Christ. So it is a mixture of what others teach us and what the Lord teaches us Himself that will lead to our maturity.

> Test number four.
>
> Are your beliefs about Jesus consistent with how He has been revealed in Scripture?

John, the Apostle, wasn't writing these words to try to catch us out. He was writing to encourage the early believers. If the Holy Spirit has truly been at work in us then we will find that our lives are now lived in a new dimension.

5

Two Keys

I believe that there are two areas of the Christian life which the Holy Spirit is emphasising, but in which the average Christian makes little progress.

Intimacy

In recent years, intimacy with God has been a recurring theme. Actually the word intimacy is not a biblical word, although it is clear what is implied. Although we are invited into God's loving presence we must never lose sight of His transcendence. Our God is different from us. Whilst we are grateful for every experience of His nearness, He remains the Lord God Almighty.

I find that there is an immediate response when the challenge to intimacy is heard. We do not need convincing that to be close to God, and to be rightly familiar with Him, is at the heart of relationship. However, even though there is immediate agreement and even desire to respond to such intimacy, how many of us can be said to be on intimate terms with the Lord?

A more biblical word that has a similar meaning is **friendship.** Abraham is described as the friend of God. An aspect of friendship is intimacy, especially those who are the closest of friends. Jesus also describes His disciples as friends in John 15:13-15. So what is it like?

Communication is at its heart
In the two instances mentioned above the Lord is sharing His heart with those who are His friends. When God is about to destroy Sodom and Gomorrah He says, *"Shall I hide from Abraham what I am about to do?"* (Genesis 18:17).

This is followed by another illustration of Abraham pleading with God for Him to save the whole town of Sodom if ten righteous people are found there. There aren't ten, but God saves his nephew Lot and his family anyway (Genesis 18:23-33).

As the disciples' friend, Jesus lays down His life for them. But alongside this He reminds them that *"everything that I learned from my Father I have made known to you"* (John 15:15). Those who are intimate with God share in God's secrets and learn His ways. The heart of God is opened to those who will draw close to Him.

Perhaps the closest of the friends of Jesus is the Apostle John who was told vital information by Him about His betrayal. John was asking who it was who would betray Jesus. Jesus replied *"It is the one to whom I give this piece of bread when I have dipped it in the dish"* (John 13:26). He then gave the bread to Judas Iscariot, and as soon as Judas took it Satan entered into him.

Attentiveness is its pleasure

The two sisters Mary and Martha both loved Jesus Christ. Both were pleased to have Him in their home. Martha was busy in the preparation of food, and grew increasingly annoyed at her sister because Mary was sitting at the feet of Jesus. She questions the Lord about whether He cares that she has been left on her own. What is so interesting is that Jesus commends Mary. *"Martha, Martha,"* the Lord answered, *"you are worried and upset about many things, but only one thing is needed. Mary has chosen what is better, and it will not be taken away from her"* (Luke 10:41-42). It is those who wish to be close to Him who will willingly and enthusiastically spend time with Him and listen to His voice.

Sharing warts and all

Jeremiah, on a few occasions, opens his heart to God in a way few of us do. Jeremiah makes it clear to God 'how he is feeling'.

> *"O Lord, you deceived me, and I was deceived; you overpowered me and prevailed. I am ridiculed all day long: everyone mocks me. Whenever I speak, I cry out proclaiming violence and destruction. So the word of the Lord has*

brought me insult and reproach all day long. But if I say 'I will not mention him or speak anymore in his name' his word is in my heart like a fire, a fire shut up in my bones."
(Jeremiah 20:7-9)

We often deny our feelings or just ignore them. We prefer to bring the best aspects of our life to Him, fearing that He won't find other parts of our nature acceptable. The person who is discovering an intimacy with the Lord also learns that he is totally accepted. He can be honest, not trying to make excuses for his sin and failures. He knows that the Lord will not reject him, but move him on to a better place.

Joy in His presence
The writer of Psalm 16 assures us that *"in his presence there is fullness of joy."* Those who are learning to remain close to the Lord, aware of their complete acceptance by Him, find that spiritual joy is an increasing reality.

This joy is not dependent on God speaking, or on a particular blessing He has given, or as a result of being used by the Lord, although all of these give their own joy. It is the joy of relationship. To be reconciled to God, and receive assurance of forgiveness and eternal life, is the perfect gift. To be close to the Lord, to place ourselves in His hands, is to have our spirits touched by Him and have joy released.

I have a friend called Veronica who has found this deep joy. She writes "I used to ask God time and time again about one part of the Westminster Confession, 'The chief end of man is to glorify God and to enjoy Him for ever.' It was the phrase 'to enjoy Him for ever' that puzzled me, but now I have seen things more clearly. For those who love God and believe His promises without question, God offers glimpses of boundless joy even while we are still on earth. As I offer my love to Father God, He fills me with His love and peace as I remain quietly in His presence. Then I experience a joy which words cannot express. I don't want to move or breathe. I don't want anything other than the joyful beauty of this encounter with the Lord God. I believe that God offers this intimacy to all His children, if only we will spend time ridding ourselves of all our cares and anxious thoughts, and reach out to Him."

It is not necessarily a joy that is obvious to all, but one that relaxes into His love, and wants to obey. Jesus makes the connection between love, joy and obedience in John's Gospel.

> *"As the Father has loved me, so have I loved you. Now remain in my love. If you obey my commands, you will remain in my love, just as I have obeyed my Father's commands, and remain in his love. I have told you this so that my joy may be in you and that your joy may be complete."* (John 15:9-11).

Dependence

The second major area is dependence on God. No one would dispute that trusting in God has its foundation in a living dependence upon him. But what does that imply?

Know your weakness
Both intimacy and dependence are foreign to our general way of life. We don't naturally live close to people and we are self-reliant. We have the correct understanding of ourselves when we know that we are weak and unable to please God in ourselves. Paul understood it when he wrote:

> *"For it is we who are the circumcision, we who worship by the Spirit of God, who glory in Christ Jesus, and **who put no confidence in the flesh**."* (Philippians 3:3)

When he speaks of the flesh, he refers to his own human nature, the self life that mistakenly thinks that it can manage without God. Paul uses a similar phrase in Romans 7:18 *"I know that nothing good lives in me, that is, in my sinful nature."* But Paul has learned to live by the power of the Holy Spirit, and is focused on the glory of Jesus Christ. However humanly strong and positive a person may be, the basis of true dependence on God is to know we are utterly weak without God's enabling. Jesus put it similarly when he said,

> *"I am the vine; you are the branches. If a man remains in me and I in him, he will bear much fruit; apart from me you can do nothing."* (John 15:5)

If things are going well or going badly, we are still weak. Our spiritual success lies in the fact that we have learnt to depend on Him in every situation.

Know how to wait on Him
The word 'wait' is a rich one in the Bible. It has a variety of meanings. To wait with hope, expectantly, patiently, in silence. At other times it has the sense of slaying the self life and humbling ourselves before the Lord.

All these are aspects of dependence. Through waiting our understanding of God is deepened, and we become more aware of what He can do. In other words as we wait on God, He reveals Himself in terms of His character and ways.

I recently spoke at a Christian convention in Pakistan. The Sialkot Convention was started by John Hyde in 1904. Hyde was known for his powerful intercessory gift, and many became Christians through his ministry. At times he would wait on God in silence for considerable periods of time in order to prepare himself to speak to God. Then he would pour out his heart with faith-filled prayer.

Waiting does not only take place when we are stationary or in prayer, but it is essentially a lifestyle that is being sought. Of course we need to set aside the time to concentrate in prayerful waiting, but it is reliance on God that needs to be cultivated. Psalm 62:1 sums it up.

> *"I wait patiently for God to save me, I depend on him alone."* (Today's English version)

Learn the way of Jesus
Three verses in John's Gospel give insight into Jesus' dependence on the Father. Jesus said,

*"I tell you the truth, **the Son can do nothing by Himself;** he can only do what he **sees** the Father doing, because whatever the Father does the Son does also."* (John 5:19)

*"By myself **I can do nothing;** I judge only as **I hear**, and my judgement is just, for I **seek not to please myself** but him who sent me."* (John 5:30)

*"When you have **lifted up** the Son of Man, then you will know that I am the one I claim to be, and **that I do nothing on my own** but **speak** just what the Father has **taught me**."* (John 8:28)

The Lord Jesus is the perfect model of dependence. When He was on earth He also lived in dependence on the Father and the Holy Spirit. In these verses He is explaining that His will and mind are absolutely at one with his Father.

We would expect this because Jesus was God in the flesh, but He was also human and so had to learn these secrets of communion and dependence. We learn three things from Jesus: relationship is crucial, His attitude is vital and His living is fruitful.

In John's Gospel especially, the Father/Son relationship is evident for all to see. Jesus breathes the same air as the Father. He is sustained by the communion that He has known from eternity past. After His incarnation as the human Jesus, the fellowship continued for He knew how *"to remain in the Father's love"* (John 15:10).

Relationship, attitude and fruitfulness

Jesus knows He can do nothing of any spiritual value without Father. We can obviously do things without God, like go to work and dig the garden, but we were made for dependence on Him in order to be holy and help others to be holy.

His chief desire is *to please the Father* and not Himself. He has a consuming passion to fulfil the wishes of the one who sent Him. Jesus' utter conviction of being sent is also a strong feature of John's Gospel. If we have conviction of what God has called us to do, then like Jesus, it should take the highest priority.

He was prepared to *sacrifice* Himself. He knew that He was to be lifted up on the cross. Here was the central part of the obedience of His earthly life. He knew that He had come to die and rise again and so His mind and attitude were fixed until this was completed. He was in agony, but with a sense of achievement. He could cry out *"It is finished"* (John 19:30).

Notice how closely Jesus follows all that the Father is saying and doing. These verses about dependence teach us about Jesus' ability to do three things well.

He *sees* what the Father is doing, He *hears* the Father accurately, and *speaks* what He has been taught. I have a friend with whom I used to work, called Gordon. He seemed to enjoy observing the way that I spoke and my mannerisms. He was able to entertain many at my expense as he 'took me off'. On one occasion he borrowed some of my clothes and glasses and greyed his hair. I even thought it was me. Dependence means we get our eyes on the Father, our ears open to His voice and have a willingness to speak out in faith what He gives us to say.

6

When Tested

Another of the questions that I asked in my questionnaire was 'What is it that you admire about another person's relationship with God?' As we might expect, most people spoke of the quality time that these people spent with God – something we have already covered in an earlier chapter. The second aspect mentioned was admiring those people who coped with suffering and responded maturely when tested.

The Devil attacks us through temptation, and according to Scripture he is permitted by the Lord to try us. We see this in the case of Job and Peter. Satan asked to strike Job and the Lord responded. *"Very well, then, everything he has is in your hands, but on the man himself do not lay a finger"* (Job 1:12). Jesus said *"Simon, Simon, Satan has asked* (literally asked permission) *to sift you as wheat. But I have prayed for you, Simon, that your faith may not fail"* (Luke 22:31-32).

The Bible teaches us that God also tests His people to deepen our knowledge and relationship with Him. God does not tempt us (James 1:13), but testing is part of His will. He does this by initiating events in our lives.

Do we fear God?

A few years after the miraculous birth of Isaac, God spoke to Abraham in a remarkable way. The language used is unmistakable.

> *"Some time later God tested Abraham. He said to him, 'Take your son, your only son, Isaac, whom you love, and go to the region of Moriah. Sacrifice him there as a burnt offering.'"*
> (Genesis 22:1-2)

What was the reason for this? Was it that Isaac had become too important to Abraham? What had begun as God's gift had now become more important than the Giver. This may have been part of it. Others reject this part of Scripture and say that Abraham was completely mistaken, because God would never ask him to do such a thing. The passage itself gives us the reason. Abraham is prevented from putting his son to death by the Angel of the Lord, and then he hears the voice of God.

> *"Do not lay a hand on the boy. Do not do anything to him. Now I know that you fear God, because you have not withheld from me your son, your only son."* (Genesis 22:12)

Notice the depth of Abraham's relationship. His fear of God had sharpened his hearing. How did Abraham know that God was now giving different instructions about Isaac? He might have held to the first instruction, because clearly he believed that if his son was killed God could raise Him up from the dead (Hebrews 11:17-19). However, Abraham knew God's voice, and understood not just the words, but the heart and nature behind it. The relationship meant that he knew when the Lord was releasing him.

We are reminded of Jesus in this passage. God also had a Son, an only Son, whom He loved, except that He did offer Him up in sacrifice for us.

What is this fear of the Lord? Someone has said "I am not afraid of God, but I do fear him." God loves us deeply and we are welcomed into His presence, so why is there need to fear Him?

It is a combination of reverence, awe and fear aroused by awareness of God. The nature and the presence of God should create in us respect and reverence which goes deep enough to include fear. This fear is not terror, but the deepest possible desire to respect, respond to, and to conform to His infinite and majestic love. The writer of Proverbs was right when he said *'The fear of the Lord is the beginning of wisdom'* (Proverbs 1:7).

What is in our hearts?

God wants to know what we will do for Him. Are our words of commitment merely words, or do we actually mean them? The years in the wilderness for the Israelites were full of trials, and therefore tremendous challenges to deepen and develop in maturity. Deuteronomy 8 tells us that God provided for them in the desert; enough food, adequate clothing and eventually a land flowing with riches beyond their imagination. But how was He to do it?

> *"Remember how the Lord your God led you all the way in the desert these forty years, to humble you and to test you in order **to know what was in your heart** whether or not you would keep his commands."* (Deuteronomy 8:3)

God wanted to see three things in their hearts. Trust in His word, co-operation with the supernatural and to submit to His discipline.

Every word from God's mouth
The Israelites were not merely to trust in the provision of the manna that fell from heaven six days a week, but to live by every word that came from the mouth of the Lord. It wasn't physical food that would ultimately sustain them, but the words of God.

Jesus also knew how to feed on these same words. When tempted by Satan to make bread from stones, He draws on His knowledge of this passage as well as His experience (Matthew 4:3-4). The words of God were spiritual food for Jesus and they fed Him at a deeper level than any ordinary bread could (John 4:32-34). The Lords want to see if His words are in our hearts and whether we choose to feed on and live by them.

I know someone who uses the Lord's Prayer as an outline for their own praying each day. When she gets to the phrase *"give us today our daily bread"* (Matthew 6:11), she will take a promise or a command of Jesus and meditate on it and take it in as a way of eating spiritual food.

His supernatural power
Such extraordinary things happened in the desert! The Israelite's

clothes did not wear out and their feet did not swell (amazing in the sweltering conditions); the manna did not stop until they reached the Promised Land and only when other food was available; the sandals they were wearing when they entered the wilderness lasted until the end. All these were supernatural signs of His Spirit.

God wants to reveal what is in our hearts. Will we live by our human strength or will we live by His Spirit? God promises signs of His power in the driest desert. We can choose to accept the wilderness experience or draw on the power of the Holy Spirit and see the Lord reveal Himself.

I know a farmer who made big sacrifices to serve the Lord which meant he gave less time to farming. He believed it was a decision the Lord wanted him to make. His potato crop that year produced a miraculous yield. It was impossible that such an area of land could produce so many potatoes.

His discipline

> *"Know then in your heart that as a man disciplines his son, so the Lord your God disciplines you."* (Deuteronomy 8:5)

Children quickly learn the word 'yes' in their dealings with their parents, but 'no' is a lot harder to accept. The truth is, if we are not sensitive to God's no's and His loving reproof, we have not travelled very far in the Christian life. It is because He loves us so much that He wants to correct us. It is the loving father who cares enough to discipline his children.

So don't be discouraged when you receive His rebuke. God is only reinforcing that you are in relationship with Him. I remember being convicted years ago by a verse in James about my poor relationship with fellow Christians (James 4:11-12). Interestingly my first reaction was to be aware of how much the Lord loved me.

What is your faith like?

God desires us *"to be conformed to the likeness of his Son"* (Romans 8:29), and one of the main ways that He uses to achieve this is the testing of our faith. Having faith is another way of describing our relationship with God. What good is our faith to us if it doesn't actively believe in someone? But God tests our faith. Life is full of trials. James and Peter speak of them:

> *"Consider it pure joy, my brothers, whenever you face trials of many kinds, because you know that the testing of your faith develops perseverance. Perseverance must finish its work so that you may be mature and complete, not lacking anything."* (James 1:2-4)

> *"In this you greatly rejoice, though now for a little while you may have had to suffer grief in all kinds of trials. These have come so that your faith – of greater worth than gold, which perishes even though refined by fire – may be proved genuine and may result in praise, glory and honour when Jesus Christ is revealed."* (1 Peter 1:6-7)

We are tested by sickness or difficult work or family circumstances. However the biggest tests come through our identifying with Jesus Christ, **when we bear His reproach**. These are the tests which reveal our faith. The sort of suffering that comes our way because we have chosen to follow Jesus. The Christians in Peter's letter were being persecuted for their faith, but Peter seizes on it as an opportunity to produce quality faith.

It is often hard to accept that all those things which life throws at us can be the means by which our faith may be purified, like gold in a furnace. The way that we grow in perseverance and maturity is by a right response to our circumstances. These trials are to be welcomed according to James because of what they can achieve.

In the main the will of God is done in the way we respond to the tests and trials that are 'our lot'. God wants to see if what we call faith in Jesus Christ is actually genuine. If it is, it will result in praise and glory to Jesus.

To paraphrase Jesus' words in John 15:18-21. He says *"Don't be surprised that the world hates you and treats you harshly. They do this because you belong to me."* It seems that the Lord allows, and sometimes initiates tests for us, because He wants an even deeper relationship with us. Let us not fail him.

❖ ❖ ❖ ❖

If you have enjoyed this book and would like to help us to send a copy of it and many other titles to needy pastors in the **Third World**, please write for further information or send your gift to:

Sovereign World Trust, P.O. Box 777, Tonbridge, Kent TN11 0ZS, United Kingdom

or to the **'Sovereign World'** distributor in your country.